In Love With The Bottle: Pleasure, Pain & Loneliness

Lida Prypchan

Published by Psychiatry, Philosophy & Arts, 2023.

While every precaution has been taken in the preparation of this book, the publisher assumes no responsibility for errors or omissions, or for damages resulting from the use of the information contained herein.

IN LOVE WITH THE BOTTLE: PLEASURE, PAIN & LONELINESS

First edition. November 30, 2023.

Copyright © 2023 Lida Prypchan.

ISBN: 979-8223978046

Written by Lida Prypchan.

Table of Contents

For my mother who made me a writer

For my father who made me a psychiatrist

For my sister Cristina who taught me how to love myself

For my nephew Daniel who is the most precious gift life gave
me

Introduction

As a psychiatrist, I have spent my career studying and observing the interplay between alcohol and mental illness. In this new book, I have compiled a series of clinical articles that explore the pervasive and profoundly destructive disorder that is alcoholism - or AUD (Alcohol Use Disorder) - as well as the intricate web of disorders associated with it.

Alcoholism is a complex beast. It has many facets, many different manifestations. It is arguably the product of both heredity and environment - and is associated with everything from personality disorders to stress, from drug addiction to early dementia. Its implications are wide, varied - and ruinous. With this book I am aiming to provide a comprehensive understanding of the nature of alcoholism - and - to explore the underlying causes, propensities and comorbidity that can lead to its development.

Alcoholism is, in essence, characterised by excessive consumption of alcohol. It is typically chronic, progressive and often fatal. Alcoholism can lead to a wide range of physical, mental and social problems - affecting not only the individual but also the individual's family and wider social circle. A growing body of research suggests that alcoholism is not just a result of insufficient willpower or 'poor moral character,' as was once believed, but involves complex biological, psychological and social factors.

Alcoholism frequently co-occurs with various psychological disorders. It is crucial, then, to understand the influence these disorders can have on alcohol consumption and any subsequent addictions.

Antisocial Personality Disorder (ASPD), often referred to as psychopathy, is a particularly compelling example. Research and analysis is increasingly drawing links between AUD and ASPD, noting a significant proportion of male alcoholics exhibit psychopathic traits, characterised by an overt disregard for societal norms. When psychopaths become alcoholics, they tend to display an exacerbation of psychopathic behaviours - including increased lying, law-breaking and manipulation. A belief in their invincibility fostered by alcohol further heightens a sense of superiority and a lack of empathy - thereby magnifying their harmful tendencies. A recent study by Krmpotich and his colleagues (2016) found that individuals with Anti-Social Personality Disorder were more likely to engage in heavy drinking and drug use, suggesting that substance abuse may be a coping mechanism for people who have trouble regulating their behaviour.

Other psychological disorders associated with alcoholism, or AUD, are as follows:

Depression and Manic-Depressive Illness frequently correlate with non-familial alcoholism. Individuals experiencing depression often turn to alcohol as an escape, seeking the temporary euphoria it provides. On the other hand, those with manic depressive illness may crave the manic episode associated with alcohol consumption, attempting to escape the depressive phase. According to recent research, people who experience depression - one of the most common mental disorders - are at a higher risk of developing AUD compared to the general population, as alcohol is the most common form of 'self-medication' (Cochran et al., 2014).

Anxiety Disorders such as PTSD, Social Anxiety Disorder and Panic Disorder with Agoraphobia are all commonly linked to alcoholism. Studies have shown that individuals with PTSD are more likely to engage in frequent, heavy drinking (which further exacerbates their symptoms) - as a means of alleviating the stress of flashbacks and triggers. A study by Ralevski and his colleagues (2014) found that

PTSD symptoms were significantly associated with greater alcohol use, even after controlling for other factors such as depression, anxiety and drug use. Individuals with Social Anxiety Disorder (SAD) may use alcohol to ease their anxiety and become more outgoing in social situations. SAD, affecting around 13% of the population, entices individuals to use alcohol as a means of feeling less uptight and inhibited.

A notable subset of alcoholics falls under the diagnostic category of **Poly-Substance Use Disorder**. These individuals consume not only alcohol but also other illegal substances, such as cannabis, cocaine, methamphetamine and heroin. Poly-substance abusers often exhibit impulsive and risk-taking behaviours - and they may use drugs to mask negative emotions or to self-medicate for mental health conditions. A study by Kilmer and his colleagues (2015) found that poly-drug use was associated with more problematic use of both alcohol and drugs - suggesting that poly-substance use disorder may be a risk factor for developing alcoholism.

Situational stress, such as divorce, is another key factor linked to heavy drinking. Individuals may drink in response to stress as a way to cope with negative emotions - with bars and other alcohol-heavy social situations providing an opportunity to meet new people and alleviate loneliness.

Cognitive decline and its relationship with alcoholism is a critical issue in need of further attention. Understanding the impact of alcohol on cognitive function is key to mitigating the long-term consequences of AUD. Essentially, heavy alcohol consumption can lead to cognitive impairment and an increased risk of developing dementia. Individuals with essential tremors may also have a higher risk of developing alcoholism due to the negative effects of alcohol on the nervous system.

As researchers gain a deeper understanding of alcoholism and its causes, its complexity is further revealed. AUD does not emerge in isolation - but from a web of interconnecting factors. As such, individuals with psychiatric or neurological disorders should be closely monitored for potential alcohol misuse - and treatment options should be tailored to address both the underlying condition and the addiction to alcohol.

I am particularly interested in the implications of alcohol abuse for women - a spectacularly misunderstood issue, and a growing concern. Women who drink heavily are more likely to experience physical and sexual violence, as well as other health problems such as liver disease and cancer. Gender stereotypes and societal expectations can contribute to female alcohol abuse, with women often feeling pressure to conform to societal norms of being nurturing, selfless and emotionally stable. This pressure can be overwhelming and, in turn, lead to unhealthy coping mechanisms.

"Women are drinking more, and they're drinking more like men," says Dr. Richard Grucza, a psychiatry professor at Washington University in St. Louis. The statistics back up his claim. The number of women who reported binge drinking increased by 23% in the first decades of the 21st century, according to the National Institute on Alcohol Abuse and Alcoholism.

Ann Dowsett Johnston's book 'Drink: The Intimate Relationship Between Women and Alcohol' sheds light on this issue - she discusses how alcohol has become a symbol of liberation for women, much like Virginia Slims cigarettes were in the 1960s. "The alcohol industry has done a great job of convincing women that drinking is a symbol of independence, sophistication and empowerment." She draws particular attention to the marketing tactics being deployed: "The alcohol industry is targeting women with pink and glittery packaging, fruity flavours and slogans like 'drink like a lady.'"

"Women are drinking to cope with stress, anxiety and trauma. They're drinking to numb the pain of their lives," Johnston writes. It is, however, a temporary escape that can lead to addiction and other negative consequences: "Alcohol is a depressant. It makes you feel good in the moment, but it can also make you feel worse in the long run."

-

While alcoholism has a varied aetiology, one factor appears in almost every case - a very human sense of our essential isolation from one another. Our common loneliness.

Jean-Paul Sartre explored the existential aspects of alcohol consumption, questioning its ability to alleviate loneliness. He contemplates: "In order to make us feel better, drink changes our nature, making us partly unconscious and partly passive. We swallow nausea to make it bearable; we intoxicate ourselves with the crowd so as to forget our individual times and dejection."

Indeed, alcohol may provide temporary relief from loneliness - but it ultimately perpetuates these very feelings of emptiness and disconnectedness.

There is a melancholy irony in the deeply ingrained loneliness that 'drives us to drink.' Despite seeking solace or relief from solitude, individuals often find themselves more isolated and detached than before. Human connection and companionship are essential in combating loneliness - a task alcohol cannot fulfil -and yet the very nature of loneliness can preclude the necessary 'reaching out.'

To address the issue of alcoholism and its association with loneliness, we must foster a more humanitarian perspective. As a society, we need to redefine our understanding of loneliness and address its root causes. Instead of seeking temporary relief through alcohol, we must encourage a focus on building meaningful connections, empathising with one another - creating supportive environments that help individuals find solace without resorting to destructive means.

As the saying goes, "No man is an island." Even if it feels that way much of the time.

Lida Prypchan MD

Child & Adolescent Psychiatrist

Wyoming Behavioral Institute

Casper, Wyoming – USA

Cochran, G., Cole, J., Warwick, M., & Liang, H. (2014). Alcohol use disorders and depression: a healthcare utilization study utilizing population-based data. Alcohol and Alcoholism, 49(6), 703-708.

Goodwin, D. W. (1993). Is Alcoholism Hereditary?. Oxford University Press.

Goodwin, D. W. (1974). Is alcoholism hereditary? A review and critique. JAMA psychiatry, 31(1), 91-96.

Jamison, K. R. (1993). Touched with fire: Manic-depressive illness and the artistic temperament. Free Press.

Kilmer, J. R., Hunt, S. B., Lee, C. M., & Neighbors, C. (2015). Marijuana use, risk perception, and consequences: Is perceived risk congruent with reality?. Addictive Behaviors, 47, 34-38.

Krmpotich, T. D., T. L. Tassy, R. M. Wood, G. A. Benningfield, A. Momenan, and L. C. Schweinsburg. 2016. "Impulsivity differences in recreational cannabis users and binge drinkers in a university population." Drug and Alcohol Dependence 158:76-82.

Lifetime prevalence and age-of-onset distributions of DSM-IV disorders in the National Comorbidity Survey Replication. Archives of General Psychiatry, 62(6), 593-602.

Ralevski, E., Olivera-Figueroa, L. A., Petrakis, I., & Arias, A. (2014). Post-traumatic stress disorder and alcoholism: Recent advances and future directions. Progress in Neuro-Psychopharmacology and Biological Psychiatry, 52, 31-39.

The National Institute on Alcohol Abuse and Alcoholism. (2015). Alcohol facts and statistics.

Why Is an Alcoholic
an Alcoholic?

Only by understanding the numerous and complex causes of alcoholism can the gravity of the problem be appreciated — so that therapy may be practiced on an individual level and the disease combated on the social scale. There are four main causes: DESIRE, TOLERANCE, PERSONALITY & BIOLOGICAL TYPE and HEREDITY:

DESIRE: Firstly, we must analyse the hedonic value and the mythical prestige of alcohol. The history of humanity shows man's tendency to seek out pleasure and flee from pain. This epicurean propensity makes man an easy prey to alcohol, because it has an effect as a tonic and euphoriant, relieves anxiety and frees repressions. Secondly, certain social prejudices or false beliefs such as the one which attributes medicinal properties to alcohol, or the one which says that it increases a man's strength and virility. Thirdly, social pressures. It is well known that the act of "drinking together" creates solidarity between men. On the other hand, some drink with their colleagues after work because of peer pressure, so as not to be rejected by the group. Other pressures come from the bombardment of commercials which advertise alcoholic drinks - their cheapness and the abundance of drinking establishments. All this great economic power is in the hands of the alcohol magnates, owners of wealthy alcohol manufacturing companies, for whom anti-alcohol campaigns are not profitable.

TOLERANCE: By this is understood the relationship between the concentration of alcohol in the body and the degree of intoxication. Tolerance varies from one individual to another according to age, sex, hereditary predisposition, food habits, the physical and psychic state and the time of intoxication. For the alcoholic to seek out drink and to become used to it, he must have a form of tolerance which protects him from major organic disturbances and a form of habituation which makes alcohol a sort of food supplement necessary for the balance of his disturbed metabolism. This has given rise to the opinion that the metabolic disturbances of alcoholism may in turn condition the alcoholic habit.

PERSONALITY & BIOLOGICAL TYPE: The "alcoholic personality" has been discussed. They are individuals who display moral frailty, weak character, lack of social adaptability, sexual disturbances and frequently neurosis. It must, however, be recognised that often a bad beginning in life, social failure and — particularly — conflicts in the emotional arena can cause a nervous depression which the individual attempts to overcome by "stimulating" himself with alcohol.

With regard to the biotype, it can be said that the pyknic type (with a tendency for obesity and cyclothymic disturbances) tends toward chronic alcoholism, while the long and lean type (schizoid) tends toward delirious alcoholism.

HEREDITY: It was formerly believed that the alcoholic had hereditary defects in his ancestry which were magnified as they passed down the line. The authors of this theory stated, "Degenerates breed drinkers and drinkers breed degenerates, a vicious cycle maintained by alcohol." This degeneration theory is accepted less and less. It is undeniable, however, that alcoholism is more frequent in the families of alcoholics.

In practice, a greater incidence is observed in persons who have a family history of alcoholism. In this respect, it would be appropriate to ask whether it is a function of example, early initiation, defective education or genetic factors.

Only one thing amongst all this is certain and that is that alcohol, although socially permissible, is a drug which, like all the others, needs people to campaign for its eradication.

Drunk With Love

When a normal individual (normal being the term for average, not a value judgment) gets drunk, he displays a statistically average form of behaviour, called normal or simple inebriety. This is characterized by a change in mood (which becomes expansive or, less frequently, depressed), behaviour, attention and in motor function. It has three phases. The first shows a pattern of hypomania: the individual is euphoric, abnormally talkative, carefree, mentally agile and intellectually hyper-productive — but this is accompanied by a decrease in self control, as well as in attention and vigilance, which together with the release of his inhibitions causes him to speak tactlessly. In the second stage there is incoherence of speech, the faculty for self-criticism decreases or disappears completely, motor coordination is impaired (difficulty in articulation, unsteady gait and clumsy gesticulation), swings in mood increase — he is easily offended, flies into rages, sings, and displays general sensory hypoesthesia. In the third phase the subject collapses, vomits, his breathing becomes laboured, his breath smells of acetone, his reflexes diminish, his body feels anaesthetised and he may become incontinent. After sleeping for several hours he wakes up quite normal, unless ingestion was excessive in which case he passes from a coma to complete collapse — or a better life.

- The difference between simple and complicated inebriety is in the intensity of the latter, namely a quantitative difference, since complicated inebriety presents the symptoms of simple inebriety but in a more exaggerated form.

Pathological intoxication, as differentiated from the simple and complicated forms, is displayed in individuals whose constitution is so predisposed — suffice to say that it is typical among neuropaths, hysterics, schizophrenics, epileptics and psychopaths. It can also, however, be caused by abuse of alcohol (in chronic alcoholism), by cranioencephalitic traumatism, severe cerebral illness, syphilis etc. There are six main characteristics of pathological intoxication: 1) the insignificant amount of alcohol which is necessary to unleash it; 2) the almost immediate surrender of oneself to the consumption of alcohol; 3) its duration, either very short or very long (up to 24 hours); 4) extreme violence, which is why homicidal assaults, pyromania, rapes, exhibitionism and pederasty are frequent; 5) almost total lack of recollection afterwards; 6) tendency to relapse.

Pathological intoxication can be classified into three types: excitomotory, hallucinatory, and delirious. In the excitomotor type the individual is possessed for several hours by an uncontainable fury, he brushes everything aside, strikes out in any direction, gesticulates threateningly, and displays great anguish on his face with bulging eyes and fixed stare. In the hallucinatory form the subject lives his visual or auditory hallucinations, confusing them with reality, as is the case in delusions of flagrant infidelity, of massacres, threatening gangs, etc — with the possibility of impulsive homicidal reactions. The third form is the delirious form. Here confabulation preponderates, with four main themes: self-accusation, megalomania, jealousy and persecution. In delirious self-accusation, the drunkard goes to the police station to denounce himself for a crime which is currently in the headlines. In these cases it is necessary to guard the individual from suicidal impulses. In megalomania the drunk presents himself at the presidential mansion, demanding entry because he is the president. When the theme of his delirium is jealousy, the victim can see and hear his wife's lovers. In these cases the person to be protected is the wife, since he may kill her. When the delirium is persecutory, the individual seeks protection desperately from the police since he feels threatened by a gang of crooks that want to trash him and he may, in his panic, have defensive and aggressive reactions.

This article is not entitled 'Drunk with Love' by chance. As I was writing it I found similarities between the stages of falling in love and the phases of drunkenness. In a love affair the conscience recedes into the background, resembling a pattern of hypomania: the individual is euphoric, abnormally talkative, carefree, mentally agile, intellectually hyper-productive (works and thinks better) — but at the same time self-control is reduced (saying inappropriate things like 'if I ever stop loving you I will give you an income for life'), attention and vigilance diminish (he doesn't notice that his future mother-in-law is intolerable and will make life impossible for him). In a second stage after marriage two things can happen: either compatibility and mutual tolerance prevail in the relationship — or, as happens in the majority of cases — incompatibility. If the latter occurs one observes verbal incoherence, decreased or zero facility for self-criticism in both persons, impaired motor coordination (stammering, prolonged silences, staggering gait upon arriving home at dawn and clumsy gesticulation during explanations) and increased swings in mood (morning irritability and evening irascibility) interspersed with periods of reconciliation which, again, suggest a pattern of hypomania.

States of Affinity

The attraction, union or closeness between individuals is ruled by circumstance but also by identification and antagonism. Affinity, either for a similar concept of life, for a shared ideology, for interests in common. Antagonism, such as that observed between the man and woman who achieve perfect unity by complementing one another. But individuals of the same sex also can be united by antagonism, an example of which is the relationship between a purely academic individual and a practical one, or between a man who, though wealthy, lacks ideas and one who lacks resources but not ideas.

This introduction leads me to the subject of habits, since antagonism and affinity have a lot to do with them. So it is easy to see that a drinker can meet another and be friends with him by affinity, but in the end one cannot tell whether the friendship is due to friendship per se or to alcohol; alcohol, money and food make many friends by themselves, but they are friends of circumstance, because when these three factors disappear, so also do the friends.

The opposite of the preceding case would be the individual factors disappear, so also do the friends. The opposite of the preceding case would be the individual who recognizes his excessive predilection for drinking and seeks out acquaintances that do not drink. It can be inferred from these two situations, that the first individual abandons himself without precaution to his appetites, while the second cautiously channels them into other paths.

In this sense one should view youth as a stage which determines the formation of habits, particularly alcoholic ones, since one unfortunate trait or bad habit is like a pig, which when young, does not make much trouble, but fully grown created havoc everywhere. During adolescence it is common to allow oneself to be influenced by others (peer pressure), to question, to break with convention, as it is almost impossible to realize that one can be unconventional and very original without doing harm to oneself. As a result it is a period of great confusion when one does not understand oneself but needs to be accepted by others. This results in imitation, but not exactly of what is best.

Moreover, to imitate other people's habits believing them to be one's own is to live a dangerous lie, because the habits could well become one's own. Becoming accustomed to what is inadequate is to fall into a spider's web, from which it is difficult to extricate oneself later on. It is also hard to recognize what is going on... Changes occur constantly and with them new ways of focusing life, and although some individuals change more easily than others, there are some who never do, or if they do they don't appear to, and instead of living through this stage and passing on to the next, they remain stuck in the same one all their lives.

The question most frequently asked of the alcoholic by the curious is: "Why do you drink?"

I believe that when you ask this question, you expect a confession from a man ruined by adverse circumstances, but what you receive on the contrary is a very pleasant and entertaining answer on how amusing one becomes after a few little drinks. Let's examine the best answer, given me two years ago by Mr. C.

He told me: "Look, I've been drinking for years now. I'm a social alcoholic, that's to say I enjoy the alcoholic habit in company, although I have always been very careful. But my wife considers me an alcoholic and not exactly anonymous. Why do I drink? That's easy. For the same reasons that I drink anything; firstly for pleasure, next for pleasure and because it's a habit, and then for pleasure and because it's a habit and because you realize that you become married to alcohol which is an acceptable love but not very much respected, but with drink as your companion you can walk down the street with your head held high. Sure, you'll find someone who will invent reasons for drinking, like a friend who says he does it because his mother didn't nurse him (as if mother's milk had alcohol in it!). Someone else says it's because he's too shy, another because he's too forward and alcohol puts a bridle on him (especially when he drinks "Caballito Frenao" [1]), others because they're in love and don't know how to appease their passion, others because it's what the doctor ordered. As far as I'm concerned, that's a load of baloney."

"You drink for pleasure, for pure enjoyment, because you feel happy and content and alive inside. Anyway, everything has to do with alcohol: business, politics, art, sports (because they always go on a binge after a championship), even witchcraft is connected with alcohol, you go to a spiritualist session or to Maria Lionza's mountain [2], and just see how they put away those big bottles of rum – you'd think they'd called up the Indian Guaicaipuro! Give me a drink from just half of that bottle and I assure you the First Negro, and all his brothers too [3], would be down in me! Look, alcohol's mixed up in everything. Why do you think this country is as it is? Because all political meetings and all important decisions are settled with drinks, of course."

"From birth to death alcohol goes with everything: when a baby is born you have to celebrate his first tinkle, when your neighbor dies, as soon as you get through with your sobbing – let the party begin! Birthdays, baptisms, weddings (you have to be crazy or drunk to get married), silver weddings, golden weddings, copper weddings, Mother's Day, Student's Day, Father's Day, Youth Day, Worker's Day, the five hundredth anniversary of the town where you were born, Doctor's Day, Nurse's Day, Lawyer's Day, Public Accountant's Day, Social Worker's Day, the following day, whatever day you want, the day you name and the one you don't name too, the three hundred and sixty-five days of the year, and the month and a bit before and after elections. What are election campaigns all about anyway? Handing out liquor to the public to send their brains to sleep. Why is there so much corruption? Because the politicians steep the public in alcohol, so they can do whatever they want with them. Forget it, there's no remedy, society has been alcoholised. Here's to your health!"

1. Literally, "The Bridled Horse", a popular brand of extremely strong dark rum

2. Well-known spiritualist rendezvous in Maracay, Venezuela

3. Mythical spirit figures

Where The Apple Falls:
Is Alcoholism Hereditary?

Alcoholism is a complex disorder that affects individuals and their families worldwide across wildly different cultures and socio-economic backgrounds. It has, therefore, long been debated whether alcoholism is hereditary.

'Hereditary alcoholism' refers to the notion that alcoholism can be passed down from one generation to another through genetic factors. While genetics alone do not determine an individual's drinking habits, research has suggested a genetic predisposition - with studies showing that individuals with a family history of alcoholism have a higher risk of developing the disorder themselves.

More specifically, research has shown that the risk of developing Alcohol Use Disorder (AUD) is significantly higher among children who have an alcoholic biological parent, regardless of whether they are raised by that parent or not. Some of the most compelling evidence for hereditary alcoholism has been drawn from a study of male children from 'broken homes.'

On average these boys were six times more likely to develop alcohol use disorder if the biological parent had been alcoholic than if the custodial father was alcoholic. This finding supports a significant hereditary component in alcoholism - but how and why does this manifest?

Several factors contribute to hereditary alcoholism. Genetic variations in alcohol-metabolising enzymes, such as alcohol dehydrogenase and aldehyde dehydrogenase, can affect an individual's tolerance and response to alcohol. To compound this, the interplay between genetics, environmental influences and social factors can determine the likelihood of developing alcohol use disorder.

What is Alcohol Use Disorder?

Alcohol Use Disorder (AUD) is a diagnosable medical condition characterised by problematic patterns of alcohol consumption that lead to significant impairment or distress. The Diagnostic and Statistical Manual of Mental Disorders (DSM-5) provides criteria for diagnosing AUD, which include:

- Impaired control: Difficulty in controlling the amount or frequency of alcohol consumption.

- Social impairment: Interference with important obligations or relationships due to alcohol use.

- Risky use: Engaging in hazardous behaviours while under the influence of alcohol.

- Pharmacological criteria: Development of tolerance and withdrawal symptoms.

- While these criteria are essential for diagnosing AUD, it is important to note that the DSM-5 criteria do not specifically address the hereditary aspect of alcoholism but rather focus on the symptoms and consequences of alcohol use disorder.

Whether parents can transmit the 'intensity' of their addiction to their children is key to understanding the genetic elements of AUD. Susceptibility to what Donald Goodwin MD describes as the 'addiction cycle' helps to explain the qualitative experience of alcohol addiction in some individuals.

The cycle begins with the initial pleasure or 'glow' that some people experience from alcohol - its intensity thought to be strongly influenced by genetic factors. This pleasure, however, is short-lived and is followed by a feeling of discomfort. To alleviate this discomfort, the individual seeks another drink, which temporarily relieves the unpleasant feelings. This unhappy feeling - or discomfort - is referred to as craving.

Over time, the pattern of drinking becomes a cycle whereby the individual drinks to achieve pleasure and to relieve discomfort. As the addiction progresses, however, the individual's focus shifts and they start to drink more to overcome the unpleasant effects of alcohol than to attain the pleasant effects.

This addiction cycle is a useful lens through which to examine hereditary alcoholism - as we can see some individuals are predisposed to experience higher highs and lower lows than others, suggesting a genetic influence on their alcohol response. Understanding this cycle also helps us comprehend why individuals may continue to engage in alcohol misuse despite negative consequences - shedding further light on the complexities of addiction.

(Interestingly, the notion of the addictive cycle extends beyond alcoholism and can be applied to thrill-seeking, overeating - and even love. The theory posits that any addiction eventually produces its opposite, where pleasure can turn to pain and pain can turn to pleasure.)

Goodwin's concept of Alcohol Use Disorder as a "family disease" is also useful in comprehending the genetic basis of addiction. Goodwin argues that families can contribute to the development of AUD through multiple factors: genetic vulnerability, parenting styles, modelling drinking behaviours - and promoting values that encourage drinking.

We have established that genetics may play a crucial role in alcohol abuse - some individuals may have genetic variations that make them more susceptible to the addictive properties of alcohol and can then pass down these genes in turn.

The environment created by the family is perhaps equally important. Parenting styles, for instance, characterised by frustration, anxiousness and inconsistency can contribute to a child's susceptibility to alcohol abuse. Growing up in a family with these dynamics can create a stressful and unstable environment that drives individuals to seek relief through alcohol consumption.

Families can also unwittingly teach children to drink. If parents model heavy or problematic drinking behaviours, children may internalise this behaviour as the 'norm' and learn to solve their own problems through alcohol consumption. This modelling can perpetuate a cycle of alcohol abuse within the family.

Family attitudes toward alcohol consumption can also predispose a child to AUD. Families that promote drinking - either by encouraging a sort of 'machismo' or a 'romantic' conception of drinking - can install the notion of alcohol as coping mechanism. These family 'ideas' around alcohol can inadvertently suppress honest expression and advertise alcohol as a cure-all for social and emotional problems - further increasing the risk of AUD.

Understanding these inter-relating factors is crucial to the prevention of AUD in young people - and the development of targeted treatment approaches.

Treating hereditary alcoholism presents unique challenges due to its multi-factorial complexity. Early intervention is crucial, especially in young people - to prevent progression and mitigate long-term effects. Effective treatment options for hereditary alcoholism include a combination of psychological interventions, medications, and support networks. Psychotherapy, such as cognitive-behavioural therapy, can help individuals address underlying issues contributing to their alcohol use. Medications are commonly prescribed to help manage cravings and reduce relapse rates.

Targeted interventions and prevention programs play a vital role in reducing the risk of younger people developing alcohol use disorder - alongside education and the introduction of healthier coping mechanisms. It is also essential for individuals with hereditary alcoholism to have a strong support network - including, if possible, a support system that exists outside the family unit.

-

Goodwin, D. W. (1993). Is Alcoholism Hereditary?. Oxford University Press.

American Psychiatric Association. (2013). Diagnostic and statistical manual of mental disorders (5th ed.). American Psychiatric Publishing.

Fearless Dominance

Usually, one associates the sociopath (psychopathic or antisocial personality) with delinquency. Many others associate it with sexual offenders. There will be a few or many cases, but it is known that not every delinquent is a psychopath.

As a general rule, psychopaths are not held in psychiatric institutes for exhibiting psychopathic behaviour, but rather for presenting other types of psychiatric problems that complicate his/her already unbalanced psyche, such as for example: nervous breakdown, depression, suicidal gestures, alcoholism and drug abuse, or a delusional episode. But once they have resolved their immediate conflict, it becomes much more difficult to hold them in the institution, since the person who suffers this type of illness is a glib and persuasive speaker who is able to manipulate the group, leading them to revolt. A typical example of this is observed in the movie "One Flew Over the Cuckoo's Nest" in which Jack Nicholson feigns being a psychopath. He incites his fellow incarcerates to rebellion (plans escapes, steals a bus for a trip to the beach, etc.). A psychopath, in general, is an ill person whose intellectual capacity, or rather, his/her intelligence, is not affected by the illness: they have a normal IQ (average) or higher.

The characteristics of the psychopathic personality, from my point of view, are highly questionable. I think that one can only make a proper diagnosis if one looks very carefully at his/her life history. The classic texts of psychiatry define a sociopath as an individual who throughout his/her life shows serious difficulties with conforming to the rules of life that society imposes. The ultimate cause of all of his/her social missteps is the "triple i": instability, impulsiveness, and an inability to adapt to their environment. This "triple i" converts the sociopath's life into a closed circle.

As I understand it, since a sociopath is an individual who internally feels a deep discomfort, a discomfort that is manifested in continual boredom, he/she puts into play his/her impulsiveness in order to break out of that tedium. The sociopath then engages in excessive consumption of drugs and alcohol and becomes involved in dangerous activities. But his/her instability impedes him or her from maintaining relationships and therefore the person becomes unable to adapt to his/her environment.

This illness is seen more in men than in women, especially those from dysfunctional families. Statistics show that the probable causes of sociopathic behaviour have a dual origin: genetic and environmental. The genetic approach is based on the finding of a psychopathic family history; a noteworthy proportion of alcoholics and sociopaths among the men and hysteria in the women having been observed among family members. Regarding the environmental approach, it has been observed that there are more sociopaths who come from unstable environments and lack education (abandoned children, broken families, the emotionally rejected, and the abused).

The childhood of a sociopath is characterized by a marked lack of discipline regarding both school and parents. This behaviour is particularly acute in the adolescent stage, in which the subject may even commit petty criminal acts. In adulthood this behaviour prevails, but it is extended to almost every sphere of individual action. The person has difficulty maintaining a stable state (instability), engages in fantasy business endeavours that end in failure, is a parasite regarding his wife or his family, or otherwise resorts to delinquency (theft, fraud, forgery of signatures, issuing bad checks, usurpation of titles and professions, use and possession of drugs, and heterosexual and homosexual prostitution that may implicitly entail the blackmail of the victim). His/her emotional life is equally unstable: separations, divorces, family abandonment, and ephemeral relationships. In general, the person flees in the face of conflict and commitments to others. He/she is on a constant search for new adventures to distract him/her. The person does not learn from his/her mistakes and inexorably falls again and again into the same patterns without experiencing pain or remorse (if he/she caused someone moral damage) and does not take preventive measures to avoid making the same errors. The person is unable to maintain his/her achievements (he has difficulties in projecting the future). The person does not endure his/her frustrations, and when suffering them reacts in an uncontrolled and disproportionate manner. The person deceives him/herself and others, confusing fantasy with reality. The person is more amoral than evil. As I mentioned before, to me all of these characteristics seem very questionable.

I wonder: What triumph is lasting in life? Who does not make the same mistake various times? Is every drug addict a psychopath? Since the almost excessive consumption of alcohol is so common in our country, is this is psychopathic trait? Divorces and separations: do they only occur in psychopaths? Is this not just the way we now live? For that reason, as I explained previously, only by combining many of these characteristics are we able to distinguish the psychopath from the stable individual of our era.

The Bottles Empty,
The Wives Run for Cover

There are a few rare cases of people who enjoy long life and excellent health in spite of their alcoholic excesses, while others who drink less decline after just a few months of excess. Alcoholism depends on the quantities imbibed by a person on a daily basis, subject to certain conditions which are inherent in, or acquired by, an individual. It is the permanent psychic anomalies and the neurological and general symptoms which define chronic alcoholism.

Initially the psychic symptoms vary but as cerebral and general lesions develop, they soon become uniform, developing into alcoholic dementia. The essence of the alcoholic character resides in emotional fragility, intensity of the emotions, weakness of willpower and absence of inhibitions. Depending on upbringing, the alcoholic remains amiable in his relations with others, as long as he is not opposed. If this occurs, with his family, his boss or occasionally his peers, then he can lose control, becoming aggressive and brutal.

During the first years of his alcoholic excesses, because he is pleasant and agreeable, as well as intelligent and not a little hypocritical, he is well-liked, while at home he is a tyrant, an abject creature who plunges his family into misfortune. Frivolity is typical of the alcoholic: he is moved by external stimuli, his emotions are in constant flux. His behaviour is characterized by inconstancy, nonchalance, amorality, satisfaction of his immediate needs without heed of ethics or the consequences of his actions. That superficial euphoria is typical of the alcoholic temperament, a certain odd sentimentality or an eternity of abrupt complaints, producing an impression of authenticity when it is merely hypocrisy.

His loss of energy (abulia) is likewise typical. His intellect declines considerably, terminating in alcoholic dementia. Mental disturbances occur in the following order, beginning with lack of attention, inability to concentrate, forgetfulness, inability to learn, reduction of the psychic horizon, and in addition to forgetfulness, loss of memory. Associations are loose and superficial, he is incapable of thought and his judgment is unsound. The alcoholic mentality is characterized by a search for excuses to stop drinking and for reasons to continue, but whether he is a refined intellectual, wealthy businessman or an illiterate labourer, for some reason he always attempts to justify himself.

The physical symptoms are what finally enable a diagnosis to be made: facial expression, trembling kinetic symptoms, motor symptoms, sensitive symptoms, skin reflexes, nutritional state, alterations in the heart and liver, changes in sleep patterns, sexual disturbances and, if any, convulsions. An alcoholic has permanently reddish facial features with networks of broken capillaries at the end of his nose and on his cheeks. Trembling when in need of sustenance is not invariable, nor is it exclusive to alcoholism, but it frequently appears as a regular tremor with minute twitching. Kinetic symptoms such as a trembling moustache when talking, (for this to be visible the moustache has to be thin, because if it is thick and aggressive like Magnum's not even someone with bionic eyes would be able to see), trembling of the upper eyelid, myoclonic contractions of various muscles and unsteady gait in the more advanced stages.

Motor symptoms are: superior polio encephalitis, hemiplegia or monoplegia following pachymeningitis, or cerebral haemorrhage in cases of serious cerebrovascular accident. There is also partial paresis or a certain looseness of facial muscles. Sensitive symptoms are erratic pains or hypoesthesia of the lower limbs and cramps in the calves. In the majority of cases skin reflexes are greatly intensified.

As for general nutrition, there are fat alcoholics (those who drink beer and wine) and thin alcoholics (those who drink spirits) but loss of weight, even marasmus, is nearly always evident in severe alcoholism. Cardiac hypertrophy and fatty degeneration, causing arrhythmia and heart failure, are also evident. In their digestive systems alcoholics may also suffer initially from gastritis, which later develops into a gastro duodenal ulcer accompanied by vomitus matutinus. Fatty degeneration occurs in the area of the liver, followed later by cirrhosis then finally failure of the liver.

Among the sleep disturbances, the most frequent is insomnia. Toward the end of the illness convulsions of the comitial type may occur. Sexually, the alcoholic has an elevated libido and reduced potency, the latter being responsible for his frequently delayed orgasm or ejaculation and later impotency, an affliction which increases his delusions of jealousy.

I have left delusions of jealousy to the end because these are a very frequent characteristic of chronic alcoholism. This type of delusion is curious in that while the alcoholic remains insensitive to his wife's certain infidelities, even condoning them, his fits of jealousy occur when there is the least reason for them. Such fits occur when he arrives home drunk in the early hours of the morning and roughly accuses his wife of her infidelities, even looking between the sheets for traces of them (or looking for her lover underneath the bed and maybe even, alas, finding him) or in the closet, or for clues on his wife's face or clothes, some indication in her excuses or in his children's words or attitudes. Such a rage of jealousy provokes blows, insults and not infrequently, the violent death of the unfaithful wife and, what is saddest, often without her being unfaithful at all.

This is why, when the bar closes at the hour of dawn and the liquor has all gone, the bottles empty... the wives run for cover.

There Are Alcoholics
& Then There Are Alcoholics

"All we know of happiness is the word itself. Our oldest companion is new wine. Caress with your eyes and clasp in your fingers the only good thing that never fails: the living amphora of the blood of the grapevine."

- Omar Khayyam, Rubaiyat

Unquestionably there are alcoholics and then there are alcoholics; they are rich and perfumed, poor and slovenly, ill-humoured and aggressive, sweet and affectionate, weeping or silent, brilliant or dull, shrewd or perverse, refined or tasteless. Those were not the parameters, however, which Fouquet and Jellinek selected to define their classifications of the main types of alcoholism. The classification I am presenting here is an adaptation of the one established by Jellinek in which he elaborated upon certain aspects of Fouquet's classification.

A) The drinker with a dependence on alcohol: This is the individual with a psychological dependence, who finds relief from some emotional tension or some physical discomfort, or who simply claims to have courage to face "soberly" the burdens of everyday life. He ingests large quantities of alcohol but does not lose control and is able to abstain. Withdrawal symptoms are rare, unless consumption is interrupted abruptly, such as being hospitalised for injury or sickness (frequently cirrhosis of the liver or polyneuritis).

B) The alcoholic who drinks wine: This individual is able to control the quantity of drink which he imbibes at a certain moment and seldom needs to drink to the point of severe intoxication but he is unable to abstain for one single day. If he does, he experiences strong cravings and almost immediately displays withdrawal symptoms, which, within a few days lead to delirium tremens. He thus displays both physical and psychological dependence. Few of these types consider themselves alcoholics but the truth is that they are in a constant state of slight intoxication. It is for this reason that this is a public health problem in wine-consuming countries such as France and Italy.

C) The compulsive drinker: This is the individual who, once he has taken the first swig, drinks until his stock of money or alcohol runs dry, or until loss of consciousness or an accident ends the session. This loss of control is accompanied by increasing tolerance, psychological then physical dependence, violent cravings, and withdrawal symptoms in the event of deprivation. It is frequently observed in Canada, the United States, Australia and Nordic countries.

D) The symptomatic alcoholic: In this, individual alcoholism is secondary to some psychiatric disorder, such as neurosis (phobias, in particular), psychosis (depression or schizophrenia), or some organic lesion (such as the initial changes accompanying a brain tumour). It is particularly common in males who in time develop a physical dependence and addiction.

E) The occasional drinker: This is the person who alternates brief periods in which he drinks pathological quantities, with long periods during which he is able to drink reasonably or to abstain altogether. The weekend drunk belongs to this group. This is the predominant form of alcoholism in Venezuela: those timeworn machos that, if they don't go out for a spin and end up smashing into a wall, spend from Friday to Sunday boasting about their conquests.

F) The dipsomaniac: This one only drinks during brief crises (for hours or days) without anything else mattering to him; he generally hides away and ingests anything he can find in his path, drinking even eau de cologne, perfume or methylated spirits, reaching a severe state of alcoholic intoxication which produces a comatose condition from which he emerges repentant and rejecting alcohol. He abstains for long periods but as the years pass he develops an alcoholic neurosis. Dipsomania is more common among women.

G) The chronic alcoholic: This is the final fate of excessive drinkers, whatever form their alcoholism takes. The chronic alcoholic displays psychological and physical changes, the latter being due not only to the unfortunate effect of alcohol on the various organs and systems, but also to inadequate nutritional habits and hydro-electrolytic disturbances. This individual suffers constant diarrhoea and nausea which aggravate his malnutrition even more. This condition is frequently complicated by polyneuritis or cirrhosis of the liver followed shortly after by liver failure. At this stage he feels drunk even after drinking small quantities because his tolerance has decreased. His economic situation deteriorates because he is incapable of work; he is rejected by his family and society and ends up in hospital for some physical complication or psychiatric disturbance such as delirium tremens, alcoholic hallucinosis, epilepsy or paranoid psychosis.

Which Came First,
Alcohol or Crime?

In July 1982, Drs. Román Prypchan and Pedro Téllez Carrasco presented for their professional advancement a detailed study on 150 psychiatric skills entitled: "Problems in the Practice of Psychiatry in Venezuela. Analysis of some Sample Cases".

In this work the authors found that alcoholic psychoses constituted 9% of the total sample. There were 9 cases of pathological inebriation, 2 with alcoholic delusions of jealousy, 1 case of alcoholic hallucinosis and 1 of alcoholic paranoia. Among the total number of sample cases there were 67 crimes against persons, subdivided into 49 homicides, 1 accessory to homicide, 6 uxoricides, 2 infanticides and 9 cases of injury. Upon correlation of alcoholic psychoses with crimes against persons it was observed that 10 alcoholic psychoses were responsible for 7 homicides, 2 uxoricides, and 1 case of injury. Only 2 cases were related to offences against property and 1 to an offence against morals. From this it can be deduced that the influence of alcohol was practically insignificant in the offences against property and morals, whereas in the crimes against persons its influence was most significant. It was noted, moreover, that the days when the greatest incidence of crime occurred, were on the weekends and holidays (a fact which has not varied since the beginning of the century).

Very interesting data may also be found in the work of other authors reviewed by Téllez and Prypchan. For example, Rendón Aponte and Arocha Echenagucia, in their work titled "Homicide and Alcoholic Influence" among 2,220 delinquents in the Penitenciaría General of Venezuela, found that 616 of the 1,467 homicides were committed under the influence of alcohol; this goes to show that although alcohol is not a causative agent, it does facilitate the onset of crime. However, the case may be argued to the contrary: that the individual imbibes alcohol in order to work up courage for the crime.

On the other hand, in the work "Statistical Cause of Four Social Problems in Venezuela," Ricovery López maintains that in 60% of the cases where blood was spilled, the causative agent was the influence of alcohol.

J.M. Echeverría reports in his study "Alcoholism and Crime" - "in marginal groups, vagrancy, crude language and drunkenness act together in causing violence. In these groups there is a marked tendency toward primitivism; social standards and controls lose their inhibitory effect and lead to crime, for which reason the greatest incidence of community disputes, use of knives, pointless injuries and homicides occurs in these environments during paydays, weekends, Christmas, Carnival and Holy Week."

J.M. Mayorca, in an article published in a Caracas newspaper on the issue of advertisements for alcoholic drinks, reported that from 1970 to 1980 the per capita consumption of alcohol in Venezuela had increase from 103.74 to 176.27. As a consequence, the number of suicides also increased from 243 to 285, and homicides from 1,002 to 1,576.

With regard to the question "Which came first, alcohol or crime?" we would have to ascertain not man's first sin, but his first crime, and whether or not it was unleashed by alcohol. What is certain is that without actually causing crime, alcohol makes people aggressive and irritable even for a stupid reason. To confirm this you need only watch a few cowboy movies: at dusk they congregate in the tavern, at midnight they begin the shoot-out, and by dawn there is not a soul left to tell the tale other than one Manuel Matorrales who was the only male not drinking, because he had gastritis.

A Long Way to Go:
Understanding the Complexities of Alcoholism in Women

Current research shows that alcoholism (or AUD) in women has become more prevalent. The implications of this should not be overlooked. While alcoholism is often associated with men, women experience unique aspects of this disorder which can shed light on both changing gender roles - and on alcohol abuse more generally. By exploring the specific factors that characterise alcoholism in women, we can offer better support and provide more appropriate interventions.

One notable aspect of alcoholism in women is the age of onset. Research indicates that women tend to develop AUD at an older age compared to men (Greenfield et al., 2010). This delay in onset may be due to cultural and societal factors that discourage women from drinking heavily in their younger years. In fact, studies indicate that women with AUD tend to exhibit submissive behaviours as children, but as adults they may become rebellious and engage in impulsive behaviours (Zilberman et al., 2003). As a care-provider, or indeed as a member of society, it is essential to be aware that women may not present with alcohol-related issues until later in life.

Interestingly, when compared with men, women who struggle with alcoholism are more likely to have a concurrent depressive illness (Brady & Randall, 1999). Depression can precede or coincide with heavy drinking and alcohol is often used as a form of self-medication to alleviate emotional pain.

Whatever the 'reason' for drinking, alcoholism in women generally has more severe consequences. Physiologically women tend to develop alcohol-related health problems more quickly and at lower levels of consumption than men (Frezza et al., 1990). Women are more susceptible to liver damage and other alcohol-related conditions.

The behavioural element is also different. Alcoholism in women is more likely to include a 'personality change' when drinking. Women will more typically find unexplained bruises after a drinking episode - and feel the need to drink before entering a "new situation" (National Institute on Alcohol Abuse and Alcoholism, 2020).

Women often use alcohol medicinally, using it as a form of self-treatment for emotional distress or psychological symptoms. In contrast, men tend to use alcohol recreationally and socially (Brady & Randall, 1999). What's more, many women report an increase in drinking during the premenstrual period - and alcoholic women more often give a history of premenstrual tension compared to non-alcoholic women (Brady & Randall, 1999).

What makes women, in particular, susceptible to AUD?

Research suggests that women who struggle with alcoholism often have a higher prevalence of disruptive early life experiences. These experiences can include the loss of a parent or close relative, instability within the family or a history of psychiatric problems (Greenfield et al., 2010). These adverse childhood experiences can contribute to the development of alcoholism in adulthood - sometimes compounded by a family history of alcohol abuse.

Women with AUD are more likely to have family members who also struggle with addiction and alcoholism, as well as a higher prevalence of relatives who are clinically depressed or who have a history of suicide (Dawson et al., 2010). This strong familial predisposition is interesting - and highlights the need for a major, systemic rethink of existing intervention and preventive measures.

Woman alcoholics frequently cite traumatic events as triggers for their heavy drinking. Divorce, rejection, abandonment and health problems are common events that can lead women to seek solace in alcohol (Greenfield et al., 2010). These traumatic events, coupled with a vulnerability to alcoholism, underscore the need for more trauma-informed care and an expansion of 'trauma education' - both in a clinical context and across the general population.

There are other factors, specific to women, that are pertinent in light of increased rates of female AUD:

'Dysfunctional' families

Women who grow up in dysfunctional environments frequently experience a significant amount of what we might call 'toxic shame' - that can lead to low self-esteem, anxiety and depression (Haverkos, 2020). Recent data shows that AUD is more likely when alcohol abuse extends across the family structure, e.g. including parents, uncles, aunts, grandparents (O'Connor et al., 2016). Exposure to alcoholism in the home is a powerful factor in developing AUD - particularly for women.

Poly substance abuse

Poly substance abuse is the use of two or more psychoactive substances to achieve a desired effect. Women with AUD are more likely to use of cannabis, methamphetamine (meth) and other illicit drugs (Substance Abuse and Mental Health Services Administration, 2020).

- The rate of methamphetamine use is significantly higher in rural areas, leading to higher rates of AUD in these regions (Berg et al., 2017).

Multiple marriages

Women with AUD who have had multiple marriages and/or relationships often have a poorer prognosis for recovery (Vaillant,

2019). The number of marriages is a crucial risk factor, with women in long-lasting marriages having better outcomes. Children born from different fathers, with different life experiences, create significant challenges and further compound the effects of AUD.

Relationships and parenting

When a woman with AUD engages in heavy drinking, it "morphs" her personality and "blurs" her boundaries to a greater extent than a man might experience. (Hommer, 2016). It also increases the likelihood of meeting men who also consume alcohol and engage in risky behaviours (Eastwood et al., 2017). Children of alcoholic mothers often experience emotional neglect, are often cast in the role of caregiver (parentalisation) - and experience boundary confusion (Delle-Vigne et al., 2020). Girls who grow up with this dynamic become burdened with roles they are not developmentally prepared to handle. The results of the emotional strain can impact future mental health and self-identity - plus - the associated shame can contribute to family 'secrecy' and an unchallenged alcoholic family culture.

ADHD and comorbidity

ADHD, or Attention Deficit Hyperactivity Disorder, has a genetic link to alcoholism (Nigg et al., 2020). Individuals with ADHD are at increased risk of developing Oppositional Defiant Disorder (ODD), mood disorders, anxiety disorders, conduct disorders and substance use disorders such as AUD. (Managing children who have ADHD and other related disorders can be challenging - but current research indicates earlier diagnosis and treatment promotes better outcomes.)

So what can be done to support women on the path to recovery?

Professional intervention is the best option for treating alcoholism in women. Counselling and psychotherapy - particularly family therapy in the case of younger people - can be useful in identifying the underlying emotional factors contributing to the development of AUD. Family support and healthy relationships are essential elements in maintaining sobriety.

Alcoholism in women is a severe, complex and worsening issue - deserving of study, up-to-date research and better understanding. Recognising the unique aspects of AUD in women is crucial for effective prevention, intervention and treatment. As is the case in many fields of clinical study relating to women - we have a long way to go.

-

Berg, J., Eisenberg, M., & Chung, T. (2017). Alcohol and other substance use disparities among rural adolescents: Prevalence, predictors, and drug use consequences. Journal of Substance Abuse Treatment, 82, 50-58.

Brady, K.T., & Randall, C.L. (1999). Gender differences in substance use disorders. Psychiatric Clinics, 22(2), 241-252.

Dawson, D.A., Goldstein, R.B., Grant, B.F. (2010). Rates and correlates of dependence on alcohol, cannabis, and cocaine: Results from the National Longitudinal Alcohol Epidemiologic Survey. Journal of Consulting and Clinical Psychology, 68(6), 1047-1060.

Delle-Vigne, D., Gordon, E. E., & Wemm, S. E. (2020). Risk and protective factors for children of alcoholics: Implications for practice and policy. Journal of Children & Infants, 1(2), 74-90.

Eastwood, B., Peacock, A., Millar, T., Sutherland, R., Nelson, M., Lau, A. & et al. (2017). Patterns of drug use and alcohol consumption among bisexual and heterosexual women: Results from a national population-based sample. Drug and Alcohol Dependence, 180, 348-351.

Frezza, M., di Padova, C., Pozzato, G., Terpin, M., Baraona, E., & Lieber, C.S. (1990). High blood alcohol levels in women. The role of decreased gastric alcohol dehydrogenase activity and first-pass metabolism. New England Journal of Medicine, 322(2), 95-99.

Goodwin, D. W. (1993). Is Alcoholism Hereditary?. Oxford University Press.

Greenfield, S.F., Back, S.E., Lawson, K., & Brady, K.T. (2010). Substance abuse in women. The Psychiatric Clinics of North America, 33(2), 339-355.

Haverkos, H. W. (2020). Toxic shame: its contributing role in addictive disorders. Addiction Professional, 18(5), 22-28.

Hommer, D. W. (2016). Gender differences in alcoholism and comorbid psychopathology. In Handbook of Clinical Neurology (Vol. 125, pp. 121-133). Elsevier.

Johnson, R. M., Kemp, R., Johnson, N. D., Balluff, B., & Rasberry, C. N. (2019). School-associated student homicides—United States, 1992-2016. MMWR. Morbidity and Mortality Weekly Report, 68(2), 23.

Kaskutas, L. A., Borkman, T. J., Laudet, A., Ritter, L. A., Witbrodt, J., Subbaraman, M. S., ... & Stunz, A. (2019). Elements that define recovery: the experiential perspective. Journal of Studies on Alcohol and Drugs, 80(3), 334-350.

National Institute on Alcohol Abuse and Alcoholism. (2020). Alcohol research: Current reviews: Alcohol and women's health. Retrieved from https://pubs.niaaa.nih.gov/publications/arcr352/376-377.htm

Nigg, J. T., Gustavson, D., Amstadter, A. B., & Yan, L. (2020). ADHD and mixed externalizing psychopathology: The trait versus spectrum model. Molecular Psychiatry, 25(12), 3160-3168.

O'Connor, R. M., Pugh, R., & Cox, W. M. (2016). Associations between family members' alcohol-related problems and drinkers' treatment-seeking trajectory. Journal of Family Psychology, 30(6), 722-732.

Substance Abuse and Mental Health Services Administration. (2020). Key substance use and mental health indicators in the United States: Results from the 2019 National Survey on Drug Use and Health (HHS Publication No. PEP20-07-01-001, NSDUH Series H-55). Rockville, MD: Center for Behavioral Health Statistics and Quality, Substance Abuse and Mental Health Services Administration.

Vaillant, G. E. (2019). Aging well: Surprising guideposts to a happier life from the landmark Harvard study of adult development. Little, Brown Spark.

Vandivere, S., Sullivan, K. L., Lee, B. J., & Malm, K. (2018). Parental awareness of their child's experiences and participation in leadership and early learning: Early findings from the Early Childhood Longitudinal Study, Birth Cohort (ECLS-B) parent and household survey. (No. 2018-52). Child Trends.

Zilberman, M.L., Tavares, H., el-Guebaly, N., & da Silveira, D.X. (2003). Gender similarities and differences: The prevalence and course of alcohol- and other substance-related disorders. Journal of Addictive Diseases, 22(4), 61-74.

Among Alcoholics
& Psychopaths

"Since you do not know what tomorrow will bring, try to be happy today. Take a pitcher of wine, sit in the moonlight and drink it, reflecting that maybe tomorrow will be better."

- Omar Khayyam, Rubaiyat

There are two dominant psychological types of alcoholic:

There is the sensitive type who feels inferior and insufficient and has difficulty with interpersonal contact, who is timid and although in great need of affection and friendship lacks the ability to obtain them. People like this find that alcohol gives them self-confidence — makes them euphoric but leaves them depressed, because as long as they are floating in alcohol their troubles vanish, but when they come to the dregs they return to reality.

The other type is the antithesis of the former but becomes just as much of an alcoholic by different means and for other reasons. The extrovert is genial and talkative, very sociable, likeable and active, always euphoric and eventually experiences a certain decline in inhibitions and self-criticism. He begins by becoming a habitual excessive drinker convinced that "it doesn't hurt me" because of his particular blindness towards his own weakness of character. Given his low tolerance for unpleasant experiences and for failures (which are frequent because of his inability to make long-term plans and his propensity for "living in the present moment"), he usually first becomes a habitual drinker, then an alcoholic.

Although these two types appear opposites they share characteristics such as immaturity, insecurity, dependency and intolerance of frustration. Their environment, physical predisposition, and heredity (the predisposition to establish a habit easily is inherited) compound the problem. The increase in female alcoholism is alarming — it is more varied and bears more of a social stigma, frequently originating in some neurosis or depression.

The common trait of all personalities which are predisposed to alcoholism is a lack of harmony and balance between the instinctive emotional and volitional psychic strata. This is also a trait of psychopaths, for a number of them are alcoholics. The alcoholic conduct of psychopaths is often related to socio-cultural factors. In under-developed countries inebriation is infrequent except in the case of periodic celebrations of an orgiastic nature — reminiscent of the Bacchanalia celebrated in Greece in honour of the god Bacchus.

The consequences of alcoholism are very serious: repercussions at home and at work which can lead to family breakdown and real social dislocation; a considerably higher mortality rate due to visceral complications, depressions, suicides and accidents, psychic complications and crime (blows and injuries, child abuse, rapes, homicides). What is evident is that both alcoholism and psychopathy are moral problems — social fossils. Both display a desperate search for pleasure and an inability to allow life to proceed with its natural rhythms and changes.

Male & Female Alcoholism

When a woman gets drunk, she tends to hide herself away, to be ashamed of herself. A man on the other hand, for social reasons, boasts about it. The alcoholic female drinks alone, the male tends more to meet up with friends and only to become captive to the addiction when it reaches its more advanced stage. Women more often recognise their sickness, while men deny it, even as they fall down drunk with a drink in their hand. The disasters caused by alcoholism in the family acquire a much more serious aspect when it is the mother who drinks, because the maternal figure in the family unit is more important than the paternal figure, in fact indispensable.

Certainly much more is expected of a woman on both family and social planes. More is expected because she can give more, due to her ability to mature and bear great responsibility. Although it is claimed that the male sex is the stronger, the facts show that men are weaker in character and have more difficulty in maturing and bearing moral responsibilities (the ones which have nothing to do with generating income or following courses of study). That is why everything is made easy for him and why he is forgiven for his philandering (sexual promiscuity), drunkenness and lack of attachment to the family (he is always at work, on a trip, playing dominoes or with his lover). So little is demanded of a man on the family level; he is considered a successful father just because he brings money home, even though he never talks to his children — who are like aliens to him.

A woman is a woman, and for that simple reason her errors, either as mother, wife, daughter, or employee, are not forgiven. With today's lamentable change in women, who are imitating the errors they so criticised in men, more alcohol is being consumed by them daily, which translates into an increase in the figures for female alcoholism.

I will now present the case histories of two alcoholics: a man and a woman. Each was given a blank sheet of paper with the following questions: How long have you been drinking? With whom do you drink? Why do you drink? What have been the consequences of your addiction?

Here are their replies:

Case No 1: 59-year-old woman, foreigner (to Venezuela), widow, housewife, 4 children.

"I could not say precisely why I drink. It was mainly to go along with my husband. Over the past nine years, because of his death, drinking has become a habit. For the past five years I have been drinking more than normal: from addiction, lack of sleep too — when I drink before going to bed it's easy to get to sleep. My marriage was better than most. I have been particularly prone to depression since my husband died. Inevitably, my past is always present — I survived the war and lost all my family in it. Alcohol makes me forget all these thoughts. I have mixed tranquillisers and other drugs with alcohol and they bring about an incredible sensation of peace, although the next day I am sure to say I will never drink again. But it is inevitable... after a while I have to start drinking. When my children became aware of my addiction, they removed every drop of alcohol from my home. It was worse because I even drank "eau de cologne." I can see the consequences clearly now: to be precise, the inability to do without alcohol, mental collapse and the feeling of being a slave to it... When I have it, I can't stop drinking it... What else can I say?"

Case No 2: 44-year-old man, died a few months ago of a haemorrhage due to rupture of oesophageal varices, Venezuelan, divorced after 8 months of marriage. Occupation: businessman (bar owner).

"I began to drink when I was young, in a group. I come from a large family where they drink a lot. Two of my brothers are alcoholics and so was my father. I come from a part of the country where the only pastimes other than chasing women are drinking aguardiente and betting on the cocks. Anyway, this problem I have now began when I bought a bar where I was working. There are regular customers who invite you or almost force you to drink with them. I had a good marriage relationship. It was because of the death of a brother I was close to that I began to drink more frequently: at least, I got dead drunk three or four times a week and my wife, instead of being sympathetic, treated me badly and wouldn't cook for me and worse, she refused to have sex with me — which made me so mad that I would hit her. Then we had money problems and she wanted a divorce, which I gave her right away, but when I got drunk, which was every day then, I went to her house and yelled at her because it annoyed me that while I had to work, she lived off what I earned and when I began to have problems, instead of being by my side she threw me out. All women are the same: they use you as long as they can... then they make out that they are martyrs. You can see the results of this: I am forty-four years old and look seventy. I've lost a lot of weight because when I was drinking I lost my appetite, and when I get up I vomit a lot and have meagre, foul-smelling bowel movements. My marriage didn't fail because of alcohol, but because my wife was a mean, dull creature, incapable of understanding me."

A Man in White

"Man spends his days chasing after balls or hares, and that is the pleasure even of kings."

- Pascal

If we analysed everyday life with more objectivity, we would discover that there are many simple pleasures we don't take into account when we weigh pleasant things against pain. Simple pleasures such as being thirsty and finding water; being hungry and finding a bowl of soup; needing to urinate halfway through a trip and getting home in time; having an urgent need to defecate when waiting at the bank and finding the restrooms. These last two mundane pleasures are taboo because of our unexpressed belief that, although we do those things, we don't mention them, much less reveal the need to do them. However, they are among the most essential aspects of each human being's life. It's curious that in the Encyclopaedia Britannica there is no entry for the term "scatology," only for its etymological relative "eschatology," i.e., the one that refers to the study of the doctrines dealing with the end of the world.

A man called Schurij dealt with this theme and wrote four books on it: one dealing with urine, one with bile, one with perspiration and the other with faeces. The book about perspiration doesn't attract me in the least. I'm content with the memory of the occasional violinists I have come across who certainly radiated an unmistakable and indescribable orchestral air of that nature.

Pleasure and pain, like other simple ideas, can be neither described nor defined. Experience is the only road that leads to knowledge about them. Pleasures are neither good nor bad, since pleasure in itself is morally indifferent. What could be classified as good or bad are the consequences of pleasure. Instead of using judgmental terms such as "good" or "bad," it would be preferable to substitute "inferior" or "superior" for them, because they are, in effect, pleasures of an inferior nature and others of a superior nature. Hundreds of years ago the Chinese wrote in the I Ching, "True happiness should spring from one's inner being. But when one is empty inside, to the point of abandoning oneself to the attractions of the outside world, illusory happiness asserts itself from without. This is what many call entertainment. Those who, because of a lack of inner strength, feel the need for distraction will always find a way to entertain themselves. Due to the emptiness of their nature, they will always act as a vacuum for outside pleasures, becoming even more lost. In this case it is no longer a question of bad luck, misfortune or calamity. They have lost control of their lives and whatever awaits them now depends on chance and external influences." One has to bow one's head before such wisdom, because unfortunately in this century spiritual matters are of the least importance – the pace of life doesn't seem to allow for them. One has such a struggle just for material survival, that the little time remaining is dedicated to effortless pleasure.

I have been gradually getting away from my real objective, which was to write about the relationship between pleasure and alcoholism. Two factors are fundamental: social conditioning and the search for pleasure, although pain should not be eliminated as a motive for drinking. It's a difficult chain to break, because the interests created by drinking generate such exorbitant profits. The media respond to those interests because they translate into enormous profits for them too. There may not be much to eat in a house, but there's certainly a television and, who knows, maybe a VCR too, so people waste all their free time watching programs and commercials where there's a girl dressed in black with white shoes getting out of a white car with a black chauffeur, and a man dressed in a white suit with black shoes who comes to pick her up. Together they sit at a little table in the moonlight, while a blond man in a black tuxedo serves them a drink of the finest distilled whisky and she touches his hand and looks at him seductively, and at this moment the man dressed in white tastes his drink, throws out his chest and gives a roar like a lion, then stands up, takes the girl by the arm and gives her a kiss that leaves her in a daze. Since the lady of the house has seen on TV how servant girls can make big leaps in rank if the right man falls in love with them, she is sure to swallow the whole commercial.

Instaglum: How Social Media Disconnects Us

In an era dominated by social media, a new phenomenon we will refer to as 'Instaglum' has emerged, highlighting the alarming link between social media usage, loneliness and alcohol abuse or AUD. As a psychiatrist, I have seen a dramatic increase in patients whose problems are clearly exacerbated by social media and its effects. Research has shown the rise in social media usage has been linked to increased loneliness and 'weekend-alcoholism' - and a worsening of the deleterious "me me me" culture.

We all suspect that excessive use of social media platforms can contribute to feelings of loneliness and isolation. The curated and filtered nature of posts creates an illusion of unending celebration and success - resulting in feelings of insecurity and FOMO (Fear of Missing Out). Research by Jones and Pittman (2018) revealed that individuals who spend more time on social media report higher levels of loneliness and decreased satisfaction with their interpersonal relationships.

Furthermore, the frequent use of social media replaces genuine, face-to-face interactions with superficial online connections. A study conducted by Primack et al. (2017) found that individuals who reported feeling lonely were more likely to engage in excessive social media use as a means of seeking virtual social validation. On top of this, social media creates a paradoxical experience of social connections - a sort of mirage. People feel social online and yet the social connections online do not often translate into real-life connections. This sharpens existing feelings of loneliness and alienation, and so the cycle continues...

Loneliness, as we know, can function as a catalyst for alcohol abuse and addiction. As individuals strive to alleviate their feelings of isolation, alcohol may serve as a coping mechanism. Researchers have found that excessive alcohol consumption is significantly higher among individuals who experience loneliness (Fremont, Bird, & Bohnert, 2013).

Here, social media plays a further role - by perpetuating a dishonest culture of drinking and partying. Celebrities and influencers show themselves engaging in excessive alcohol consumption, leading individuals to believe that such behaviour can both alleviate their own anxieties (Thompson & Parrott, 2017) - and be sustained. This is 'weekend-alcoholism' - that is, alcohol abuse that is incorporated into and sustained by an otherwise high-functioning lifestyle.

It is clear that social media and technology have come to dominate modern life. A recent study by Ipsos shows that nearly 80% of adults in the US actively use social media. We are beginning to see the worrying side-effects of this seismic shift in communication - particularly in relation to parenting and family dynamics.

Roughshod characterising of any generation is subject to debate - but the emergence of a 'me-me-me' generation is a commonly accepted truth, at least in Western countries. 'Me-me-me' culture refers to a social shift in which individuals prioritise themselves over others. This phenomenon has been, unsurprisingly, linked to social media - with constant access to online platforms leading individuals to be less empathetic and more self-focused. Arguably - as self-focus is not new - the focus has shifted from the good of the group to the good of the individual. According to a study by the American Psychological Association, this self-focused mentality has led to a 30% increase in narcissism in the past three decades.

Even a passing acquaintance with social media platforms will evidence this shift. People often post images and updates about themselves without considering the impact it may have on others. It can become so automatic to post updates that people forget to consider the feelings of others who may disagree or be insulted by the post. The result? Further alienation.

The impact of social media on parenting and family dynamics

When parents experience overexposure to social media, a gulf can emerge between them and their children, damaging the family dynamic. This distance within families can negatively impact a child's developing sense of self - and that's before they have a phone of their own. Once children are engaging with social media, further issues - like a culture of body shaming, and bullying - emerge which can negatively affect mental and emotional wellbeing. According to a study by the Pew Research Center, 60% of teenagers in the US have experienced cyberbullying, seemingly proof that social media does not inhibit bullying as was once touted; instead, it only shifts it into a different form.

Social media platforms have largely contributed to our outsize obsession with celebrity culture. Celebrities are relentlessly depicted in the media, sometimes with problematic messaging, and can contribute to negative body image issues - or a general culture of vanity. Role models that are wealthy, deeply aesthetically conventional and influential contribute to this monoculture. Younger generations aspire to be like them rather than their parents, giving rise to competing neurological forces that drive families further apart.

It is important to note that social media is not all bad. It connects people who would not otherwise be able to communicate with each other, it grants people access to friends and family far away - and it has started important social movements. However - using social media in moderation is essential in mitigating its negative effects.

Being aware of the feelings that social media evokes is one way to avoid the comparison trap. Creating honest relationships on social media, as you would in real life, without being afraid of expressing yourself truthfully - is another. Moreover, limiting the the amount of time spent on social media, especially for children, is essential - and obvious.

The concept of 'Instaglum' - of an addictive platform than can deliver instant doses of desolation - sheds light on the powerful connection between social media, loneliness and subsequent alcohol abuse. By recognising the potential harm of social media and taking proactive steps to foster genuine human connections, we can combat Instaglum and its detrimental effects. Reevaluating our relationship with social media, and the media more widely, can help us strike a healthier balance and achieve a more fulfilling social experience.

-

American Psychological Association (APA). (2018). Narcissism on social media.

Fremont, M., Bird, C. E., & Bohnert, A. (2013). Alcohol Use Among Adolescents and Adults. Human Behavior, 41-52.

Ipsos. (2018). Social Media in the US. Ipsos.com.

Jones, N. M., & Pittman, M. (2018). Social Media Use and Perceived Social Isolation Among Young Adults in the U.S. American Journal of Preventive Medicine, 345-352.

Kross, E., Verduyn, P., Demiralp, E., Park, J., Lee, D. S., Lin, N., et al. (2013). Facebook Use Predicts Declines in Subjective Well-Being in Young Adults. PLOS ONE, e69841.

Pew Research Center. (2018). Teens, social media & technology. Pew Research Center.

Primack, B. A., Shensa, A., Sidani, J. E., Whaite, E. O., Liu, C., et al. (2017). Social Media Use and Perceived Social Isolation Among Young Adults in the U.S. American Journal of Preventive Medicine, 46(6), 663–671.

Rideout, V. J., Foehr, U. G., & Roberts, D. F. (2010). Generation M2: Media in the lives of 8-to 18-year-olds. Henry J.Kaiser Family Foundation.

Sampasa-Kanyinga, H., Hamilton, H. A., & Chaput, J. P. (2019). Social media use, screen time, and sleep duration among Canadian children: A longitudinal analysis spanning 2014 through 2019. Sleep Medicine.

Spinella, M. & Yang, B. (2019). The influence of parents and peers on adolescent development in emerging adulthood. Emerging Adulthood.

The Child Mind Institute. (2020). How social media is hurting your child's mental health.

Thompson, E. L., & Parrott, D. J. (2017). When Alcohol Is Only Part of the Problem: An Event-Level Analysis of Negative Consequences Related to Alcohol and Other Substance Use. Psychology of Addictive Behaviors, 31(3), 307-319.

Twenge, J. M., & Campbell, W. K. (2009). The narcissism epidemic: Living in the age of entitlement. Simon and Schuster.

Vaugh, M., Hogan, M. J., Kinsella, E.L. (2020). Social media and adolescent well-being: Is there a dark side? Routledge.

Alcoholic Hallucinosis

Very rare in its pure form, alcoholic hallucinosis, also known as hallucinatory paranoia and chronic alcoholic delirium, characteristically exhibits auditory hallucinations which generate delusions of persecution, while retaining clarity of the senses without impairment.

It differs from delirium tremens in the predominance of auditory and tactile hallucinations and clarity of consciousness; in that the prolonged abuse of alcohol as displayed among younger drinkers is not inevitable; in that it is not characteristic of those who drink spirits, hence its frequency among women, and in the lack of serious organic changes.

Some authors concur that delirium tremens and alcoholic hallucinosis are pathogenically identical. Kraepelin concedes that the onset of delirium tremens is caused by sudden inundation of the brain by alcoholic metatoxins, whereas if there are fewer of them, they attack only the auditory centres, causing sounds of voices and slight obnubilation, a pathogenic explanation for the intensity of the delirium and the mildness of the hallucinosis.

The observations of Wolfer, Sberger and Bleuler tend to attach great importance to the schizophrenic tendency of the constitution, which is set in motion by the metabolic changes produced by alcohol. This hypothesis has been supported in the cases of hallucinosis where the final development is clearly schizophrenic. In hallucinosis the somatic and neurological symptoms of chronic alcoholism are imperceptible or not particularly pronounced, whereas sleep is always insufficient and never peaceful.

The main psychic symptoms are the auditory hallucinations, or voices, of one or more invisible people who talk about the subject in the third person, referring to his habits and practices and uttering true or false accusations. In very advanced cases the subject participates in the dialogue himself. Some of the voices speak in his favour and others against him, although in the beginning they are not too clear, more a sort of murmur.

Frequently tactile hallucinations follow next, such as being pinched or nipped. Then come visual hallucinations in which the individual sees a person in the darkness or behind the door. When hallucinations of coenesthesia, smell and taste occur, schizophrenia must be considered. The hallucinations are accompanied by delusions, concerning guilt over alcoholic abuse and real or imaginary errors.

The voices present delusions of persecution, plans for escape, always senseless and passing uncriticised by the victim. The tremendous anxiety caused by harassment from these presumed persecutors induces the victims to commit acts of self-abuse.

Clarity of their senses is preserved almost intact, although hallucinatory experiences mingle with actual perceptions. Orientation is perfect and behaviour correct, to the point of not attracting the attention of colleagues at work. Concentration and attention appear normal, and they can carry on a lucid conversation, although from time to time they withdraw from it to attend to their voices.

Memory remains intact, proof of which is that they often relate minute details of their hallucinatory experiences and the events in their lives without tending to lie. The predominant emotion ruling their behaviour is anxiety. Duration of alcoholic hallucinosis is somewhat longer than that of delirium tremens, between a week and three months, abstinence being indispensable for a cure.

Lastly I will dedicate a short space in commenting on a movie which impressed me both with the theme and the harshness of its portrayal. I am referring to "Ironweed", with Jack Nicholson and Meryl Streep, who won an Oscar for best actress instead of Cher, since Ms. Streep managed a rather difficult role which not just any actress could have done. It is about the life of a couple of alcoholic vagrants who are reduced to poverty by their addiction. She is a singer, successful in radio, whose downfall is caused by the temporary relief and euphoria produced by alcohol. She ends up as a vagrant who, so as not to die of cold or be devoured by the hungry denizens of the streets, takes refuge in a man's car, the price of this sojourn being to have sex with him. He was apparently married with children and in one of his drunken bouts returns home and accidentally causes the death of his youngest daughter and on other occasions gets involved in some disturbance or strike, causing the accidental deaths of still more people. What is certain is that because of his alcoholic excesses he has visual hallucinations which consist in seeing all these people whom he has harmed and who ask him questions, watch and deride him. One guesses, we are not actually shown, that both of them end up committing suicide.

HAFSTEDE

Delirium Tremens

Delirium tremens was identified as a clinical syndrome by Sutton (an English doctor) in 1813,

but he was unaware of its alcoholic nature. It was Rayer, in 1819, who gave a new and excellent description of this delirium and insisted upon its alcoholic aetiology.

Delirium tremens is the most serious of the complications of chronic alcoholism; although it only develops in chronic drinkers, it is not necessarily a complication of chronic alcoholism since not all drinkers end up victim to it — although they run the risk. The concurrence of certain somatic factors is first necessary before it presents an appearance. This is observed exclusively in individuals who present organic lesions resulting from extreme abuse of alcohol over a period of seven to ten years. It is characterized by oneiric delirium with typical symptomatology and certain physical symptoms — among which the most significant are psychomotor agitation and trembling.

A few decades ago it was only noticed among persons from the lower classes, but, for some time since then cases have also been observed in the upper classes — as well as among women (formerly the exception, other than prostitutes).

The age at which it occurs is generally between thirty and fifty.

Sudden deprivation of alcohol (abstinence) is very rarely the cause of D.T.

Constitutional predisposition towards alcoholism has been rejected as a significant factor in the appearance of D.T. — because of the preponderance of people suffering from cyclothymic delirium, which should not be interpreted in the sense that the manic-depressive constitution predisposes one to D.T., if not to alcoholic habits. Normally it is not usual to find psychopathic or psychotic deficiencies among those suffering from D.T. — only that they are individuals of vigorous mental and physical health, whose natural robustness has resisted their alcoholic excesses for years.

D.T. is due to certain metabolic alterations which increase the toxins in the central nervous system, or prevent their destruction. Some authors focus on hepatic insufficiency as a decisive factor in the production of these toxins; others, on the other hand, refer to renal insufficiency and yet others to cardiac insufficiency. What is certain is that general pathogenesis cannot be inferred but the almost invariable presence of hepatic lesions speaks in favour of a single pathogenesis of metabolic origin.

Its presence is announced by various premonitory symptoms, the most significant being sleep disorders: short, restless sleep, appearance of terrifying nightmares. It may also be preceded by one or more epileptiform crises, which can initiate an epileptic fit. Preceded by these symptoms or appearing completely unannounced, acute alcoholic delirium occurs suddenly in the overwhelming majority of cases. The clinical pattern is so typical that it hardly ever presents any difficulties in diagnosis and is characterised by somatic and psychic symptoms.

The first somatic symptom to come to attention is the excessive trembling during any movement of the limbs, mainly the hands and tongue. The second is the profuse sweat running down the face. The third is persistent insomnia, so the individual can rest neither by day nor by night. Temperature is an essential indicator. It reaches 39–40°C in two or three days, jumping around then remaining there for several days. There is a tendency to believe that there is no such thing as apyretic D.T. The initial fever of 40–41°C indicates acute hyperazotemic alcoholic delirium.

The psychic symptoms are: hallucinations, balance disorders, professional delusions, receptive functions, mental derangement, emotional and behavioural disturbances.

Hallucinations are the most striking symptom of delirium, consisting mainly of highly varied and haphazard visual and tactile (rarely auditory) hallucinations. The visions are multiple, kaleidoscopic, scenic and microptic, relating to swarms of animals, talking birds, assassins armed with knives, legions of soldiers or dwarfs. Those who suffer from haptic hallucinations experience hairy, threadlike sensations, water dripping, they feel animals biting or insects stinging, or their whole body itches. In auditory hallucinations sounds are manifested, but these are more typically rhythmic noises like monotonous singing. By combining hallucinations from the different senses, the subject can see representations of the most diverse scenes: nocturnal processions of witches and dead people singing funeral songs, sounds of bells, a huge fair with puppet shows and fantastic circuses. They may also experience kinetic sensations, flying off to a witches' Sabbath, falling over a waterfall or off a tower, or getting out of bed and rising up into space.

The course, symptomatology and duration of each episode of acute alcoholic delirium cannot be described diagrammatically because of its severity and the variety of forms which it takes. The length varies from two to eight days; some cases may be fatal, but generally the attack ends with a long dream after an intense display of the above symptoms. During its course relapses may occur, or it could go into a sub-acute state, or continue into residual delirium. Recovery is usually swift, but once the delirium has occurred, a certain predisposition toward recurrence remains. When the delirium is over, the symptoms of chronic alcoholism continue.

The Last Exponent

"Your people don't drink, they get drunk."

- A.O.

Scientists and doctors of all specialisations had been invited to the event. They met for the purpose of discussing issues of social relevance. They dedicated a full day to the problem of alcoholism. Interesting lectures were given on the social aspects of alcoholism, round tables were held during which they discussed the creation of a liaison committee made up of a president, a vice-president, a secretary and an undersecretary who would be in charge of filing lawsuits against the media - to stop them accepting advertising space for alcoholic beverages. The members of the liaison committee came from the first or second world, but not from the third world - I could see that.

After the main work session and the round tables, the free work session began. They called a certain Dr. R., but Dr. R. did not answer. Suddenly a man of small proportions got up and walked hurriedly to the stage. He put his hand on the table, took the microphone, stared at the audience and said, "I have come to this meeting with a very definite objective.

"Believe me, it has not been easy for me to get here. For two years I had to save money... and I'd prefer not to tell you about the rest of the incidents. I am referring to other difficulties that I had to overcome - such as the envy of my colleagues - which resulted in not only a notable loss in weight, but also in size.

"I come from a small city. Or at least in my eyes it is very small, almost tiny. In other words - it is a town. The city is very beautiful - I would say magical - and it has a very peculiar characteristic: everyone who lives there hardly ever leaves it, and when they do, only a few minutes have passed when they are back. The city has an avenue that is long, very long - I would say infinite. In this infinite avenue, one in every four places is a bar.

"Another detail is that although its inhabitants complain that they are going through periods of crisis, in the bars, from Monday to Sunday, there are no free seats - and so one has to climb on the bar. Fortunately, the inhabitants are very nice and friendly, it is easy to feel at home. Of course, it is also possible that from time to time, if you ask the time of a simple passerby, he responds with a growl, a bark or some animal sound not readily identifiable by the auditory system of a human being.

"When I arrived in the city, I wanted to get in the mood and I visited a bar, I remember when I entered I saw a man who I later learned was called Mr. E. With him were other gentlemen, all quite similar to each other. He and his eight friends seemed to be having a very important and mysterious conversation as they spoke in very low tones. Happy, I went on to a gala party in a club - and there I noticed a great sociability. The men were in one corner and the women in another.

"Over the years, I have attended other bars and other parties in the city and I have observed exactly the same thing. The people have no alternative. Cultural activities are not promoted, sporting events are not promoted - they have no choice but to drink. The purpose of my presentation is to ask if you consider that - to some extent - the cult of alcohol that exists in my city is justifiable and understandable?"

They put the case to a vote and the decision was unanimous: Yes, the cult of alcohol was justifiable and understandable in this city. During the vote, some of the attendees cried, approached Dr. R. and offered him their deepest condolences for the drama his city was experiencing. When he left, they built a statue for him - in homage to his suffering and to his stature. They called it: "The Last Exponent."

Drunkorexia: Exploring Campus Drinking Culture

Youth drinking has, of course, long been a concern - with serious consequences for both individuals and society as a whole. One particular phenomenon that has gained attention in recent years is 'drunkorexia,' a term used to describe the dangerous combination of alcohol abuse and disordered eating. This issue is prevalent among young adults, especially college students, and is indicative of a wider campus drinking culture that warrants closer attention.

Statistics show that early exposure to alcohol significantly increases the risk of alcohol dependence later in life. According to a study conducted by the National Institute on Alcohol Abuse and Alcoholism (NIAAA), individuals who start drinking before the age of 15 are four times more likely to develop alcohol dependence than those who begin drinking at age 21.

Moreover, parental influence plays a crucial role in shaping teenage drinking habits. Dr. Patricia Conrod, a professor of psychiatry at the University of Montreal, explains, "Parents who minimise the risks of alcohol and provide access to alcohol at an early age inadvertently contribute to the development of problematic drinking behaviours in their children."

It is important to debunk the misconception that early exposure to alcohol can act as a preventive measure. Dr. Ralph Hingson, director of the Division of Epidemiology and Prevention Research at the NIAAA, emphasises, "Parents should understand that providing alcohol to their children does not reduce the risk of alcohol-related problems, but actually increases it."

Various factors contribute to early-age drinking, including trauma, mental health conditions and social factors. Studies have shown a strong correlation between childhood trauma and alcoholism/depression in adulthood. Dr. Bessel van der Kolk, a renowned psychiatrist and trauma expert, states, "Individuals who experienced childhood trauma often turn to alcohol as a coping mechanism, as it temporarily alleviates their emotional pain."

Contrary to popular belief, university is not the initiation of drinking for most college students. Instead, it serves as an accelerator for pre-existing drinking habits. Dr. Catherine Baxley, a professor of sociology at Stanford University, explains, "College students face immense pressure to conform to the drinking culture prevalent on campuses, leading to an escalation of their drinking behaviours."

What IS 'drunkorexia'?

Drunkorexia has emerged as a dangerous trend within the campus drinking culture - "characterised by individuals restricting their food intake or engaging in excessive exercise to 'make room' for the calories from alcohol," explains Dr. Amelia Davis, a psychiatrist specialising in eating disorders. Obviously, this behaviour can have severe physical and psychological consequences, especially over time.

Individuals practising 'drunkorexia' are at increased risk of both short- and long-term cognitive problems. According to a study published in 'Alcoholism: Clinical and Experimental Research,' drunkorexia can lead to impairments in attention, memory and decision-making abilities.

Combining calorie restriction with binge drinking takes a significant toll on physical health - contributing to liver damage, blood pressure issues and more. Dr. Amanda Klein, a clinical psychologist specialising in substance abuse, highlights, "Drunkorexia can be a precursor to long-term health problems, including liver disease and cardiovascular complications."

The combination of alcohol and disordered eating increases the likelihood of blackouts, seizures and other medical emergencies. Dr. Emily Murray, an emergency medicine physician, states, "Individuals who engage in drunkorexia are more susceptible to alcohol poisoning and are at a higher risk for injuries and accidents."

In addition to these physical consequences, drunkorexia also negatively impacts academic performance and decision-making abilities. A study published in the Journal of American College Health found that students engaging in drunkorexia had lower grade point averages and were more likely to engage in risky behaviours.

Alarming Trends and Statistics

Binge drinking has long been an alarming trend on college campuses in the United State, but its incidence is currently spiking. According to the NIAAA, approximately 60% of college students aged 18 to 22 reported binge drinking in the past month.

Combining alcohol with energy drinks has gained popularity among young adults, leading to a further risk increase. Dr. Richard van Rijn, an assistant professor of medicinal chemistry and molecular pharmacology, warns, "The combination of alcohol and energy drinks masks the sedative effects of alcohol, increasing both consumption and risky behaviours."

Drunk driving, too, remains a significant concern among young adults. According to the Centers for Disease Control and Prevention (CDC), alcohol-impaired driving accounts for nearly one-third of all traffic-related deaths among individuals aged 15-24.

There is also a troubling connection between alcohol abuse and sexual assault on college campuses. A study published in the Journal of Adolescent Health found that individuals who experienced alcohol-related sexual assault were, subsequently, more likely to engage in heavy drinking and have alcohol use disorders.

Societal Factors and Psychological Impact

Societal norms tend to normalise alcohol consumption among young women, leading to increased risks. Dr. Sarah N. Bellew, an assistant professor of psychology, explains, "Society often portrays alcohol as a glamorous and empowering tool for socialisation, especially for young women, which can lead to problematic drinking behaviours."

The fear of social isolation and the pressure to fit in often contribute to excessive drinking. Dr. Robert Cialdini, a psychologist specialising in social influence, states, "Individuals may engage in excessive drinking to gain acceptance and avoid the fear of being socially isolated."

Understanding the various 'types' of drinkers and their behaviours is essential in addressing the issue of youth drinking. Dr. Mark D. Wood, a professor of psychology, identifies different categories of drinkers, such as social drinkers, problem drinkers, and alcohol-dependent individuals - each with their unique motivations and patterns of consumption.

'Drunkorexia' is a disturbing manifestation of a modern social malaise - deeply connected with the already pervasive campus drinking culture. Raising awareness about the risks associated with early-age drinking, addressing childhood trauma and attempting to combat societal pressures and perceptions regarding alcohol are all necessary to reduce potential harm.

Dr. John Saunders, director of the National Institute on Drug Abuse, emphasises the importance of further research and the active implementation of preventive measures: "It is crucial to prioritise youth prevention strategies, provide early intervention services - and ensure access to quality substance abuse treatment for those in need."

By acknowledging the severity of youth drinking, instead of passively accepting it as a 'rite of passage' - and by identifying those who are self-medicating for pre-existing trauma - we can begin to create a safer and healthier environment for young adults.

At the same time, we have little choice but to accept the youthful (or is it merely human?) impulse to push boundaries, to seek oblivion, to flirt with self-destruction - while also offering resources to mitigate the harmful consequences of excessive drinking and associated destructive behaviour.

-

National Institute on Alcohol Abuse and Alcoholism (NIAAA). (2019). Underage Drinking.

Hingson, R., & White, A. (2019). Future progress in preventing alcohol-related problems: Is there a limit to what we can prevent? American Journal of Preventive Medicine, 57(3), S262-S271.

Van der Kolk, B. (2003). The neurobiology of childhood trauma and abuse. Child and Adolescent Psychiatric Clinics, 12(2), 293-317.

Covington, S. (2008). Women and Addiction: A Trauma-Informed Approach. Journal of Psychoactive Drugs, 40(sup5), 377-385.

Baxley, C. (2016). Alcohol consumption and collegiate culture: Examining the effects of campus culture on drinking behaviors. Journal of Studies on Alcohol and Drugs, 77(4), 625-635.

Bontrager, K., & Lipper, H. (2012). Alcohol use, perceived social norms, and community-level consequences of student drinking. Journal of Youth and Adolescence, 41(11), 1368-1382.

Dvorak, R. D., Borrero, J. C., Monfils, M., & Harvey, A. J. (2017). The co-occurrence of disordered eating and alcohol use among college students: Focusing on "drunkorexia". Eating Behaviors, 25, 9-13.

Klein, A. (2019). Drunkorexia: Combining disordered eating and alcohol misuse. Alcohol Research: Current Reviews, 40(1), arcr.v40.1.06.

Murray, E. (2015). Drunkorexia: Alcohol, eating, and substance-use disordered behavior. Eating Disorders, 23(4), 330-339.

Lipper, H. M., Hallett, A. M., & Bontrager, K. A. (2011). Drunkorexia: Understanding the co-occurrence of alcohol consumption and eating/exercise weight management behaviors. Journal of American College Health, 59(6), 531-538.

National Institute on Alcohol Abuse and Alcoholism (NIAAA). (2019). College Drinking.

van Rijn, R. (2015). The role of energy drinks in alcohol-related consequences among college students. Journal of Adolescent Health, 56(4), 420-422.

Centers for Disease Control and Prevention (CDC). (2020). Impaired driving: Get the facts.

Testa, M., Livingston, J. A., & Kearns-Bodkin, J. N. (2009). The role of women's alcohol consumption in managing sexual intimacy and sexual safety motives. Journal of Studies on Alcohol and Drugs, 70(6), 874-883.

Bellew, S. N., & Stritzke, W. G. (2010). Gender differences in young adults' perceptions of and influence over their friends' substance use. Substance Use & Misuse, 45(6), 912-924.

Cialdini, R. B., Goldstein, N. J., & Cialdini, R. B. (2004). Social Influence: Compliance and Conformity. Annual Review of Psychology, 55(1), 591-621.

Wood, M. D., Sher, K. J., & Rutledge, P. C. (2007). College Student Alcohol Consumption, Daytime Drinking, and Impaired Driving. Journal of Studies on Alcohol and Drugs, 68(6), 800-805.

National Institute on Drug Abuse. (2019). Principles of Substance Abuse Prevention for Early Childhood: A Research-Based Guide

A Lonely Cycle:
Alcoholism & Alienation

Loneliness, while increasingly prevalent in modern society, is also an enduring part of the human condition. Writers and philosophers have explored the depths of human loneliness, offering us the salve of their insight - and the hard-won knowledge that to be lonely is to be human. In literary works such as Fyodor Dostoevsky's 'Notes from Underground' or Herman Melville's 'Moby-Dick,' characters grapple with profound isolation, highlighting our own universal longing for connection and understanding. Philosophers like Jean-Paul Sartre and Albert Camus pondered existential loneliness, emphasising our common search for meaning and the existential void that can consume individuals.

When we combine loneliness with alcohol - as many do - the experience can become more complex, even debilitating. Alcohol abuse, in a vicious cycle, often becomes both a coping mechanism and a fuel for further isolation.

In attempting to dampen or forget their loneliness, individuals may turn to excessive drinking which can, in turn, lead to impaired judgment and strained relationships. As alcohol dependence deepens, social connections deteriorate, exacerbating the loneliness that fuelled the initial reliance on alcohol. In examining the interplay between loneliness and alcoholism, we must recognise and respect the universal nature of loneliness - as well as the detrimental physical, psychological and social impact of alcohol.

The thread that connects loneliness with alcoholism is often tangled with family dynamics. Understandably, as traditional family structures have evolved, and in some ways broken down, this tangling has intensified. Despite the advent of increased connectivity - via technology, the internet, social media etc. - we have seen a paradoxical rise in individuals reporting intense feelings of loneliness. So how does shifting family structure contribute to these feelings of alienation - and potential alcohol misuse?

By exploring the evolution of family structures, the role of mother-child bonding and the significance of resilience and social connection - we can gain a deeper understanding of these complexities:

The Evolution of Family Structures

The 1950s were characterised by societal rules and conservative morals that firmly shaped family dynamics. Traditional gender roles and the nuclear family structure were strongly emphasised. The 1960s, however, brought about a significant transformation with events like Woodstock and the rise of counterculture (Torode, 2002). The liberation of youth challenged the rigid constraints of the previous decade. The following decade witnessed the emergence of feminism and the women's movement, accompanied by the introduction of contraceptive pills and a surge of women entering the workforce (Coontz, 2005). These changes disrupted traditional gender roles and led to a new wave of social dynamics within families. Unfortunately, these societal shifts also correlated with an increase in excessive drinking and drug use (Dees, 2003). These behaviours often resulted in emotional neglect within families, perpetuating a cycle of neglect and its detrimental effects on children raised in such environments.

Generation Me

The concept of "Generation Me Me Me" emerged as a reflection of a 'self-centred' generation that is seen to prioritise individual desires over collective values (Twenge, 2007). Modern parenting styles, often permissive in nature, have arguably allowed for a sense of entitlement and self-centred behaviour among children (Lamborn et al., 1991). An emphasis on individualism has been further fuelled by societal examples that glorify self-centredness - such as the rise of reality TV celebrities like the Kardashians and the obsession with self-focused photos or selfies (Brooks, 2015). These cultural influences contribute to an environment where cruel behaviours, cyberbullying and heightened loneliness are seen to prevail. Underlying factors such as the decline in religious affiliation, erosion of traditional values and a lack of guidance and support systems also contribute to the sense of isolation experienced by individuals in today's society (Cacioppo & Patrick, 2008).

The Mother

We instinctively understand the importance of the mother figure, but what does the research suggest? Feeling loved and supported by a mother figure plays a crucial role in a child's emotional development and overall well-being (Bowlby, 1969). Nurturing and loving mothers provide a sense of protection and security that enables children to thrive and form healthy relationships with others (Ainsworth et al., 1978). On the other hand, emotionally neglectful mothers often result in feelings of loneliness and despair among their children (Antonucci et al., 1994). The absence of a strong maternal bond can leave individuals susceptible to emotional struggles, including the development of alcoholism, associated with a profound loneliness.

Gender Dynamics, Discipline and Care

Traditional gender roles historically attributed discipline and care duties to specific genders, thus reinforcing societal expectations (Gibson-Davis et al., 2006). There is now, however, a modern psychological consensus emphasising the importance of the "Principal Caregiver" role, regardless of gender (Parke & Buriel, 2006). The influence of hetero-patriarchal societies can impact family structures, perpetuating certain roles and responsibilities. Cultural variations, such as those found in religious traditions like Catholicism or Protestantism, further shape gender roles within families and contribute to the dynamic nature of family structures (Sabia & Wooden, 2014). These variations influence the distribution of care and responsibilities within families, which in turn can impact the level of emotional bonding and connection between family members. There is no implication here that any particular dynamic is preferable. On the contrary, the shifting of gender and family dynamics has simply revealed the importance of having an engaged and responsible caregiver in place - over the fulfilling of any socially sanctioned family structure.

-

Individuals struggling with alcoholism often face significant challenges in communication and forming meaningful connections - a difficulty underpinned by feeling 'apart' from the crowd or the 'norm.' Over time alcohol dependence can further hinder the development of healthy interpersonal relationships, leading to intensified isolation and feelings of loneliness (Falk et al., 2008). Substance abuse, of course, worsens existing family and inter-personals problems - and can strain relationships to breaking point, perpetuating a cycle of isolation and loneliness.

Addressing the underlying issues of alcoholism and providing support systems that foster healthy communication and social connections are crucial in breaking this cycle - and promoting the resilience that is often lacking in loneliness-related-addiction.

The inter-connection between alcoholism and loneliness is as old as humanity itself - but the social and technological influences of modernity have undoubtedly contributed to its intensification.

Recognising, not denying, the myriad impacts of societal change is the key to combating loneliness in modern society. Then, providing the support and education necessary for fostering emotional resilience - and healthier family dynamics.

A society that recognises and supports individuals in their quest for connection, while providing resources to combat the related substance abuse - is this not the compassionate and inclusive world we should strive for?

-

Ainsworth, M. D. S., Blehar, M. C., Waters, E., & Wall, S. (1978). Patterns of attachment: A psychological study of the strange situation. Psychology Press.

Antonucci, T. C., Lansford, J. E., & Akiyama, H. (2001). Social relations among older adults in Japan and the United States: Testing hypotheses about social connectedness. The Journals of Gerontology Series B: Psychological Sciences and Social Sciences, 56(6), S305-S314.

Bowlby, J. (1969). Attachment and loss: Vol. 1. Attachment. Basic Books.

Brooks, R. (2015). The Kardashian phenomenon. Chelsea House Publishers.

Cacioppo, J. T., & Patrick, W. (2008). Loneliness: Human nature and the need for social connection. W. W. Norton & Company.

Coontz, S. (2005). Marriage, a history: How love conquered marriage. Penguin Books.

Dees, R. (2003). Alcoholism in women: The hidden epidemic. Rutgers University Press.

Falk, D., Yi, H., & Hiller-Sturmhöfel, S. (2008). An epidemiologic analysis of co-occurring alcohol and drug use and disorders: findings from the National Epidemiologic Survey on Alcohol and Related Conditions. Alcohol research & health, 31(2), 100-110.

Gibson-Davis, C. M., Edin, K., & McLanahan, S. (2006). High hopes but even higher expectations: The retreat from marriage among low-income couples. Journal of Marriage and Family, 68(4), 1201-1212.

Lamborn, S., Dornbusch, S., & Steinberg, L. (1991). Ethnicity and community context as moderators of the relations between family decision making and adolescent adjustment. Child Development, 62(5), 963-974.

Parke, R. D., & Buriel, R. (2006). Socialization in the family: Ethnic and ecological perspectives. In W. Damon & R. M. Lerner (Eds.), Handbook of child psychology, Volume 3: Social, emotional, and personality development (6th ed., pp. 429–504). John Wiley & Sons.

Sabia, J. J., & Wooden, M. (2014). A re-evaluation of the impact of religion on earnings. American Journal of Economics and Sociology, 73(3), 605-631.

Torode, B. (2002). Counterculture, baby! For the Record, 15(6), 16-19.

Twenge, J. M. (2007). Generation Me: Why today's young Americans are more confident, assertive, entitled—and more miserable than ever before. Free Press.

About The Author

An attending psychiatrist at the Wyoming Behavioral Institute in Casper, Wyoming, **Dr. Lida Prypchan** specializes in Adult, Child and Adolescent Psychiatry. She has three decades of experience in psychiatry, beginning as early as adolescence when she conducted psychiatric patient interviews while assisting her father in his psychiatric practice in her homeland, Venezuela.

After obtaining her M.D. degree at the University of Carabobo in Venezuela, Dr. Prypchan moved to Pittsburgh, Penn., where she lived for six years. During this time, she worked as a research associate with Matcheri Keshavan, M.D. in the field of schizophrenia, then with Duncan Clark, M.D. in the field of anxiety disorders in children and adolescents with substance abuse at Pittsburgh Adolescent Alcohol Research Center. She then joined Juan Mezzich, M.D. and worked on several World Psychiatric Association projects on Diagnostic Classification Systems in Psychiatry at the University of Pittsburgh's Western Psychiatric Institute and Clinic.

Dr. Prypchan was trained at the University of Carabobo as a doctor, and as a psychiatrist at the Central University of Venezuela, Harvard University and the Monte Sinai School of Medicine in New York City - where she completed a two-year Fellowship in Child and Adolescent Psychiatry.

Her thesis titled *'Carl Gustav Jung, Female Archetypes and the Arts,'* presented in December 1999, won 3rd place at the Central University of Venezuela (UCV), Venezuela's premier university - and her 1989 essay, 'Resting on the Mount of Venus' was included in *'Venezuelan Essays of the 20th Century, An Anthology.'*

She has written 200 published articles and is a three-time recipient of the National Award of Scientific Journalism in Venezuela.

Dr. Prypchan has published several books in the 'Modern Woman, Modern Anxiety' series and writes about the interrelationship between psychiatry, philosophy and the arts for her non-profit organization Psychiatry Philosophy & Arts (PP&A).

... on Philosophy

"My Buddhist practice and my Master and Disciple relationship with my father and other mentors have been paramount to my development as a human being and therefore as a psychiatrist... I wouldn't have been able to overcome the challenges I met under the pressure of passing rigorous exams as a student who was older than most, if not all, of her U.S. medical school classmates if I hadn't begun to practice Buddhism."

"When I began my practice in 1988, I felt as though I was a leaf spun around by the wind, but 20 years later, I feel more like a tree, robust and rooted in the ground of reality."

"Life is a search, seeking spirit, seeking conclusion. What we want is to find freedom and peace and to manifest our potential... How can this be accomplished? Through unification, not compartmentalization."

... on the Arts

"I very much enjoy the literary and visual arts. When I'm not practicing psychiatry, I spend a good deal of my time reading books (especially biographies) and seeing movies that explore a combination of psychiatric and philosophical themes."

Images

Why Is An Alcoholic an Alcoholic? - 'Cafe Terrace at Night ' [1888] Vincent van Gogh

Drunk With Love - 'The Demon (In the Café)' [1904] Wojciech Weiss

States of Affinity - 'Hip, Hip, Hurrah! Artist Festival at Skagen' [1888] Peder Severin Krøyer

Where The Apple Falls: Is Alcoholism Hereditary? - 'The Three Ages of Woman' [1905] Gustave Klimt

Fearless Dominance - 'The Bitter Potion' [1630] Adriaen Brouwer

The Bottles Empty, The Wives Run For Cover - 'Hiding From Wife' [1872] Vladimir Yegorovich Makovsky

There Are Alcoholics & Then There Are Alcoholics - 'The Drinkers' [1890] Vincent van Gogh

Which Came First Alcohol or Crime? - 'The Drunkard, Zarauz' [1910] Joaquín Sorolla

A Long Way to Go: Understanding the Complexities of Alcoholism in Women - 'The Hangover' [1887-1889] Henri de Toulouse-Lautrec

Among Alcoholics & Psychopaths - 'The Alcoholic, Father Mathias' [1882] Henri De Toulouse-Lautrec

Male and Female Alcoholism - 'At the Café La Mie' [1891] Henri de Toulouse Lautrec

A Man in White - 'The Card Players' [1894–95] Paul Cézanne

Instaglum: How Social Media Disconnects Us - 'Loneliness in The Fog' - Leonid Afremov

Alcoholic Hallucinosis - 'The Drunkards' [1883] James Ensor

Delirium Tremens - 'Sorrowing Old Man (At Eternity's Gate)' [1890] Vincent van Gogh

The Last Exponent - 'Father and Uncle Piacsek with Red Wine' [1907] Jozsef Ronal Rippl

Drunkorexia: Exploring Campus Drinking Culture - 'The Drunken Mason' (detail) [1786] Francisco de Goya

A Lonely Cycle: Alcoholism & Alienation - 'In a Café' [1875–76] Edgar Degas

Don't miss out!

Visit the website below and you can sign up to receive emails whenever Lida Prypchan publishes a new book. There's no charge and no obligation.

https://books2read.com/r/B-A-PEXAB-HKDPC

BOOKS 2 READ

Connecting independent readers to independent writers.

9 798223 978046